ESCAPING POVERTY

Escaping Poverty

AND OTHER THINGS YOU MAY NOT HAVE BEEN TAUGHT

Bobby Kearan

PayBAK

Contents

Introduction   1

1 Everything you need to know is in the First Chapter   5

2 Secure a Stable Job   9

3 Prioritize Health   23

4 Home and Auto Maintenance   41

5 Managing Debt and Savings   49

6 Invest in Quality   58

7 The Education Barrier   65

8 The Other Things   70

9 Addendum - Math   90

Introduction

The Unspoken Lessons of Life

Growing up, my household had an unusual dynamic. Through no choice or consequence of my own, I found myself under the care of my grandparents. Now, don't get me wrong—their wisdom was extensive, and the love they bestowed upon me was immeasurable. They carried the torch of our family traditions and imparted countless life lessons. However, with an extra generation between us, there were gaps in their teachings. Some subjects remained untouched, not due to neglect but simply because they were either unfamiliar or uncomfortable territories for them. This book aims to bridge those gaps for individuals facing similar circumstances—whether raised by older guardians, a single parent, without parents, or by parents/ guardians who may struggle with self-care, let alone the challenging task of caring for and guiding another person.

Between my high school graduation in 1990 and my first real job in the Information Technology (aka "IT") field in 2004, my career path was a tapestry of diverse roles. I explored positions at video rental outlets, worked the night shift at gas stations, and faced the daily rigors of warehouses from unloading trucks to operating the man-up fork trucks to pull inventory to load into the semi trailers. My skill set expanded with stints as a security guard, navigating the highways as an over-the-road truck driver, and working as a stockman and occasional cashier at a prominent retail establishment. My trajectory into the tech world was charted when a friend offered me an opportunity to join them at a telecommunications and alarm company. This pivotal role laid the groundwork for my deepening interest in IT. After my initial experience at the telecommunications and alarm company, I explored opportunities with other firms in the same industry. Moving on, I collaborated with a real estate developer and ventured into the sector by working alongside a real estate broker. Steadily pursuing my interests during this period, I simultaneously undertook various contract IT roles. Fortune favored me when one such IT contract position, facilitated by the contract company, transitioned into a long-term temporary assignment. Demonstrating my skills and commitment, this temporary role eventually culminated in a permanent IT position in 2004. I embraced this opportunity, dedicating myself to the role, and remained with the organization for just over nine enriching years.

I'm sharing these words not just as someone reflecting on my own past but as someone who's observed a broader story in our society. I've watched many people, friends, and family, face challenges as they tried to improve their lives in the circumstances they were born into and the places they grew up. I really want to make a positive difference or, at the very least, assist others in achieving more success in breaking free from the grip of poverty. In today's world, which is fast-paced and always changing, a lot of older folks are finding themselves working long past the age they thought they'd retire. They often take jobs that don't match their skills and experience, not because they want to stay active but because they have no other choice. Even with programs like Social Security that are supposed to help, many seniors are barely getting by. The main problem at the heart of this struggle is that they didn't have enough knowledge about money, finances and retirement savings and thus missed out on opportunities when they were younger that could have helped them build a secure financial future.

In our current conversations, we often hear about the significance of what parents teach their children, sometimes even more so than what they learn in school. However, the reality is quite clear. Many kids are growing up in households where one parent is absent. In some cases, the caregivers, overwhelmed by the struggle to make ends meet, may not have the time or knowledge to pass on these vital life lessons. The idea that "it's the parents' responsibility" leaves out all the children born into or living in homes that don't meet society's affluent, two-parent, one bread-winner, outdated standard. This viewpoint is just one example of the systemic bias against those who are less fortunate.

This work isn't an indictment of caregivers or parents who don't meet those outdated standards. On the contrary, it's a testament to their resilience and strength. However, it's essential to recognize and address the voids left by circumstances, generational gaps, or societal changes. Whether it's understanding the nuances of digital technology, grasping the importance of mental health, or navigating the intricacies of financial planning, there are myriad areas where those responsible for teaching the young may not have had the exposure or information to guide the next generation adequately.

Thus, through the pages of this book, I aim to shed light on those unspoken lessons, the ones that many of us had to stumble upon or learn the hard way. My hope is that the subsequent chapters will serve as a beacon, allowing readers to grasp concepts more effortlessly, sidestep pitfalls, and ascend to financial stability and personal fulfillment. Let's embark on this journey together, rewriting our narratives, and ensuring that the generations that follow have a clearer, smoother path.

"Everybody is a genius. But if you judge a fish by its ability to climb a tree, it will live its whole life believing that it is stupid."
- Matthew Kelly attributes this to Albert Einstein, but nobody can find where the genius wrote such a thing.

1

Everything you need to know is in the First Chapter

We often hear that money doesn't buy happiness. While this holds a kernel of truth, it's also undeniable that financial stability provides a solid foundation from which to pursue happiness. In the dance of life, money plays a rhythm that dictates many of our moves. Therefore, understanding how to manage, save, and invest money wisely can make all the difference between a life filled with financial stress and one of comfort and security.

Let's start with a simple principle: Your income should always exceed your expenses. In essence, ensure you're not spending more than you're earning. It sounds straightforward, yet many fall into the trap of living beyond their means. An easy-to-remember guide that can assist here is the 50/30/20 rule. Picture your income as a pie that's divided into these three slices:

50% Essentials: This portion of your income should be dedicated to the basics – food, clothing, housing, and transportation.

30% Finances: Think of this as the slice of the pie that safeguards your future. Allocate this to paying off debts faster and padding your savings.

20% Self-Care and Mental Health: While some label this as 'entertainment', it's essential to view these expenses as investments in your well-being and overall happiness. This might include leisure activities, hobbies, or even a vacation.

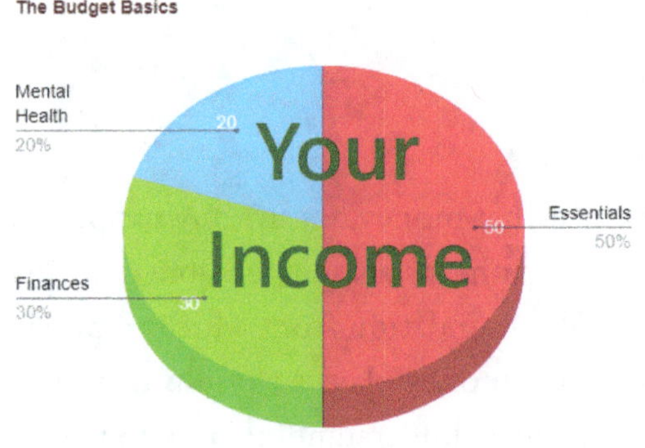

Now that we've outlined the core principle let's delve deeper:

Secure a Stable Job: The job market can be daunting, but your goal should be to secure a position not only aligned with your skills and passions but which also offers room for growth and advancement. Over time, this can significantly impact your earning potential.

Prioritize Health: A healthy body and mind are invaluable. Regular medical and dental check-ups can prevent more costly issues down the line. Additionally, focus on holistic health— ensure adequate sleep, maintain a balanced diet, and incorporate regular exercise. Remember, investing in your health now can save you a significant amount in future medical bills.

Home & Auto Upkeep: Much like how we schedule regular check-ups for our health, our homes and vehicles also need consistent maintenance to stay in top shape. Whether it's clearing out those gutters, getting that oil changed, or simply checking tire pressure, these seemingly small tasks can help you avoid costly repairs down the road. It's well worth your while to arm yourself with some basic maintenance know-how. Thankfully, there are plenty of online resources and community workshops that can help you learn these essential skills. The choice is simple: invest a little in maintenance now, or potentially pay a hefty sum for repairs later.

Debt Management and Savings: It's incredibly tempting to embrace the convenience of credit cards, personal loans, and various forms of debt that promise immediate gratification. But it's crucial to exercise restraint and minimize your reliance on these financial tools. When you do use credit, strive to pay off the full balance every month to steer clear of those burdensome interest charges. Your top financial priorities should be two-fold: first, build a safety net of savings equivalent to at least two months' worth of expenses. Secondly, start saving for retirement as early as possible – you can even open your own IRA to get started on this journey! And keep in mind, the choice of where you save matters too; consider opting for a credit union that offers competitive interest rates for your hard-earned money.

Invest in Quality: Whether it's a pair of shoes, a gadget, or even groceries, quality often trumps quantity. It might seem cost-effective to always go for the cheaper option, but quality items tend to last longer, proving to be more economical in the long run. The age-old saying "buy it nice or buy it twice" rings true here.

In conclusion, navigating the financial maze of life can feel overwhelming, but with a structured approach and discipline, you can lay the foundation for a secure future. By understanding the value of money and its effective management, you're not just ensuring your financial well-being but also paving the way for peace of mind and genuine contentment.

For more resources and links, visit : https://bak9.net/EPR

2

Secure a Stable Job

Understanding the Dream and Reality

Growing up with my grandparents in rural Mississippi taught me a lot, but there were gaps in what they could impart. My aspirations, even in high school, veered towards Information Technology (IT). Yet, being 17 miles outside a small town without consistent transportation was a daunting obstacle, and we couldn't afford a computer. My early challenges, combined with my limited knowledge about resources like local libraries or high school-provided resources, slowed my career trajectory. The lament of "nobody told me" is not just an excuse but reflects the harsh realities many face. How do you ask about what you don't know exists? Especially when your situation feels hopeless - nobody knows how to escape!

**Applying for a Job can be
Intimidating**
BK via NightCafe AI

Breaking Down the Process to Secure a Good Job

1.   Pre-Employment Requirements: The Catch-22 Situation

Often, to secure a job, you need to present yourself well, which requires money. This can be a perplexing Catch-22. Having access to basic necessities such as clothing for interviews, maintaining personal hygiene, and being able to communicate effectively are critical. You need a job to earn, but you need to spend to be job-ready.

Standing at the doorstep of an awaited job opportunity, you're greeted with an ironic challenge. While the job promises financial stability, stepping through that door requires resources you might not yet possess. To look employable, there's an inherent cost involved, but without a job, how can one bear these expenses? Lets start with the challenges that are faced.

1. Appearance and First Impressions:
   We often hear that first impressions are lasting. This holds particularly true for job interviews, where, unfortunately, appearances matter. Clean, professional attire that aligns with the role you're applying for can make a significant difference. But quality clothing doesn't come cheap.

2. Personal Hygiene:
   Good personal hygiene not only boosts your confidence but is also a basic expectation in professional settings. This encompasses regular showers, groomed hair, brushed teeth, and clean nails. While these may seem like basics, maintaining them requires resources: from toiletries to perhaps even access to clean water or a decent barber.

3. Effective Communication:
   One could argue that possessing the skills for a job should be enough. Yet, the ability to communicate these skills effectively is absolutely crucial. How is a prospective employer supposed to know of your exceptional skills unless you tell them? Sometimes, this might mean investing in courses or attending workshops to enhance your communication or interview techniques.

4. Investing in Tools:
   Depending on the job, you might need to showcase a portfolio, present a project, or offer samples of your work. These require tools, software, or materials, which, again, come at a price.

So, how does one break free from this circular predicament of how to prepare for a job, without having a job?

Start Small, Think Big:
If you're constrained by a tight budget, consider thrifting. Second-hand shops often carry quality clothing at a fraction of the price. Some cities even have specific organizations that provide interview attire for those in need.

Community Resources:
Leverage local resources. Libraries, community centers, and non-profit organizations often offer free or low-cost workshops on communication, resume writing, and interview skills. They might also provide resources for personal grooming or hygiene.

Network:
Reach out to friends, family, or community members. Sometimes, a simple ask can lead to borrowed clothing for an interview or a shared resource that can help you prepare better.

Barter and Exchange:
In a community or network, consider bartering skills. Maybe you can fix someone's computer, and they can help you with interview preparations or lend you a professional outfit.

Online Resources:
The digital age offers a plethora of online resources. Websites offer free courses, YouTube has countless tutorial videos,

and platforms like LinkedIn provide tips on effective job hunting and networking.

Recalling my early days, I was blindsided by these unexpected pre-employment costs. The journey from the rural outskirts of a small Mississippi town to a professional environment was paved with challenges, one of which was this very Catch-22 situation. However, with a mix of resourcefulness, and sheer determination, I, like many others, eventually found ways to navigate it. I hope these pages help you find how to navigate your particular challenges quicker and less painfully than it took me.

The essence lies in understanding that while the system poses challenges, there are always workarounds. The key is persistence, adaptability, and a bit of creative thinking. After all, every job interview is not just about showcasing your skills but also your ability to problem-solve, and what better way to prove it than overcoming the very challenges that stand between you and your job?

2. Identifying Your Strengths and Interests:

First and foremost, recognize what excites you. But how does one get there? By being honest about your strengths, and seeking roles aligned with your passions and capabilities. We all have an internal compass that gravitates toward certain interests and passions. For some, it's a melody that compels them to music; for others, it might be the mysteries of the universe that pull them towards astrophysics. For me, it was the intricate, vast universe of Information Technology (IT).

How does one discover and fine-tune these interests?

1. Self-Reflection:
   Take a moment to delve deep within yourself. What activities or topics make time fly for you? When you're engrossed in something, what is it usually about? These questions can guide you towards understanding your intrinsic motivations and passions.

2. Experiment and Explore:
   You don't truly know your affinity for something until you dip your toes in it. If you're drawn to a field, take up related hobbies, read books or articles about it, or join relevant clubs or groups. For instance, before diving into IT, I tinkered with computers, explored software, and read every related article I could get my hands on.

3. Seek Feedback:
   Share your interests with friends, family, or mentors. Sometimes, outsiders can provide valuable insights into your strengths. Maybe you're good at explaining complex subjects, indicating a strength in teaching or training. Or perhaps you have a knack for understanding technical nuances, hinting at a potential career in a technical domain.

4. Analyze Your Achievements:
   Your past successes can be a mirror to your strengths. Reflect on your achievements, both big and small. What skills or attributes did you utilize most? Recognizing these can be pivotal in understanding your strong suits.

5. Formal Assessments:
   Consider taking aptitude or strengths assessment tests.

Tools like the StrengthsFinder or Myers-Briggs Type Indicator can provide structured insights into your capabilities and inclinations.

6. Envision Your Ideal Day:
Imagine a regular workday in your life ten years from now. What are you doing? Who are you interacting with? How do you feel at the end of the day? This mental imagery can often help outline what truly resonates with you.

In my journey, realizing my draw to IT was only the beginning. The path to truly embracing it required acknowledging my strengths, aligning them with my passion, and then relentlessly pursuing opportunities in that domain. And remember, while it's beneficial to identify a field that excites you, it's equally crucial to be adaptable and open to change. Your strengths and interests can evolve, and that's completely natural. Embrace the journey of self-discovery and let it guide your career trajectory.

3. Information Gathering:

You must take charge of your situation and education. Talk to guidance counselors, reach out to businesses involved in your field of interest, and seek internships - paid or unpaid. Companies can offer great learning experiences if you just ask. But remember, simply knowing that you need to ask is half the battle.

Information is scattered, often overwhelming, and the real gems? Well, they require a bit of digging. Knowing you need to ask is a great start, - but ask Whom? What, exactly, to ask? When is the time to ask?

1. Be Proactive:
   Adopting a motivated mindset is crucial. Passivity may lead you to missed opportunities and lack-luster growth. Remember, doors don't always appear open; sometimes, you need to knock, or even give a little nudge, before they will reveal the treasures inside.

2. Leverage School Resources:
   Your educational institution, be it high school or college, is a gold mine of resources. Guidance counselors are there to help guide your academic and career trajectory. Engage with them, ask questions, and discuss your aspirations. They often have information on courses, workshops, and internships tailored to your interests.

3. Reach Out to Businesses:
   Identify businesses or professionals in your field of interest. Don't hesitate to reach out. Whether it's a brief informational interview, shadowing a professional for a day, or just an informal chat over coffee, these interactions can provide invaluable insights. These professionals were once in your shoes and can offer both guidance and cautionary tales.

4. Internships - A Stepping Stone:
   Internships, whether paid or unpaid, offer a real-world taste of what a job entails. It's a chance to apply your theoretical knowledge, understand workplace dynamics, and network. Even if the role isn't exactly what you had

in mind, the experience can be illuminating. Remember, every job role, even the seemingly mundane ones, teaches you something. Be it a new skill, patience, teamwork, or simply the art of making coffee!

5. Always Ask:

This can't be stressed enough. If there's something you want to know, ask. If there's a role you want to understand better, ask someone who does it. If there's a workshop or seminar you wish to attend, ask if there are scholarships or fee waivers. It might feel daunting initially, but remember, the most successful people have often been the ones who weren't afraid to ask questions.

6. Continual Learning:

The world is in a constant state of flux. Industries evolve, job roles transform, and skills that are relevant today might be obsolete tomorrow. Stay updated. Attend workshops, take online courses, join forums or groups related to your field, and keep that thirst for knowledge alive.

In my personal journey, I often lamented, "Nobody told me." But with time, I realized that the onus was on me to seek, to question, and to explore. My problem was that I didn't know, or even hope, that there were other opportunities available, or even that they were out there. The wealth of information I gathered not just shaped my career but also enriched my personal growth. Remember, knowledge isn't always handed over on a silver platter; sometimes, you need to carve your own path to it. So, wear your explorer's hat and step into the world, armed with curiosity and determination.

4. Tackling Logistical Barriers: Transportation and Location

Having the right skills is one thing; being able to reach the job is another. Especially in remote or underserved areas, transportation is crucial. If you lack personal transportation, explore ride-shares, public transit, or even relocation close to job hubs.

Broke and Broke Down - again
BK via NightCafe AI

1. Assess Your Personal Transportation Situation:
   Do you own a vehicle? Is it reliable for daily commutes? If the answer is yes, you're off to a good start. However, if the vehicle isn't available, ensure you have a backup plan. Sometimes even those with personal vehicles might find it more cost-effective to resort to other modes, especially in cities where parking or congestion charges are high.

2. Dive into Public Transit:

   For many, public transit is a lifeline. Buses, trains, subways, and trams have been connecting potential employees to workplaces for decades. Familiarize yourself with the local transit system - timings, routes, and fares. Seasonal or monthly passes often come at discounted rates, making daily commutes more affordable.

3. The Rise of Ride-Shares:

   Apps like Uber, Lyft, and local counterparts in many countries have revolutionized daily commuting. They offer a convenient, often cost-effective alternative to traditional taxis or owning a personal vehicle. Some of these apps also offer carpools, allowing you to share rides with fellow commuters, further reducing costs.

4. Consider Relocation:

   It might sound drastic, but for some, relocating closer to job hubs or more urban areas can be a game-changer. While there's a cost associated with moving, the long-term benefits - reduced daily commute, savings on transportation costs, and more job opportunities - might make it worth the consideration.

5. Flexible Work Schedules:

   If your job permits, explore the possibility of flexible work hours. Commuting during non-peak hours can be quicker and less stressful. Similarly, some employers now offer remote work options for certain days of the week, significantly reducing the transportation challenge.

6. Networking and Community Solutions:

   Engage with colleagues, neighbors, or community

members. Often, local communities have informal ride-share groups or carpool systems. Not only does this address the transport challenge, but it's also a great way to build relationships and integrate into your community.

7. Prioritize Proximity during Job Searches:

When searching for jobs, consider the location as a critical factor. If two opportunities are equally attractive but one is significantly closer or better connected via transit, it might be the more practical choice in the long run.

In my early days, I vividly recall the challenges of living on the outskirts of a small town in Mississippi, miles away from any significant employment hub. The feeling of being 'so close, yet so far' was palpable. But as with all challenges, it taught me the value of adaptability and perseverance. Where there's a will, there's a way - or in this case, a ride!

So, as you embark on or continue your professional journey, remember to plan not just for the role but also for the route. The road to success is, after all, made up of many actual roads, paths, and transit lines.

5. Embracing the Evolution of Your Career:

Not everyone gets their dream job on the first try. My career meandered through various roles before I found my fit in IT. Each role, though not the dream, offered lessons. Remember, these experiences, even if they feel like detours, are adding to your skill set.

Building Long-term Professional Success

1. Professional Etiquette: The Unsaid Rules

   Once in a job, adhere to professional norms. Dress appropriately for your role, maintain regular personal hygiene, be punctual, and communicate effectively. Small behaviors can make or break perceptions.

2. Continuous Learning and Improvement:

   Securing a job isn't the end. Continuously seek feedback, identify areas of growth, and upskill. If your employer offers on-the-job training or opportunities for further learning, seize them.

3. Recognizing the Need for Change:

   While loyalty is valuable, recognize when it's time to move on. If you consistently deliver yet see no upward movement or rewards, consider other opportunities. However, when leaving, be respectful. Give ample notice and ensure a smooth transition.

4. Planning for the Future:

   While managing daily tasks, don't lose sight of the future. If your job offers benefits such as a 401k with a matching contribution, maximize it. Think of it as a nest egg you're building for your retirement.

In summary, navigating the job market, especially when starting from a place of generational poverty, isn't straightforward. It requires grit, perseverance, and continuous learning. However, with the right steps and resources, success isn't just a dream; it's achievable. I hope my journey, with its peaks and troughs, serves as both inspiration and a practical guide for those on a similar path.

3

Prioritize Health

When we discuss the complexities of navigating the realms of health and wealth, it's reminiscent of treading through a challenging maze. Both are crucial pillars supporting the edifice of a fulfilling life. These pillars often appear at odds, especially when resources are limited. But with a refined perspective, one can discern that investing in health can lay the groundwork for a prosperous future.

The unfortunate reality for many in financially constrained situations is the necessity to prioritize one immediate need over another. The allure of cheap, easily accessible, and often unhealthy food choices becomes an ingrained habit. To truly pave the way out of this cyclic trap, a seismic shift in priorities is required. Let's take a deeper look at staying health on a budget:

1. The Power of Rest:

    Why: Sleep is the foundation for optimal brain function,

emotional balance, and physical stamina.

How: Aim for a consistent sleep schedule, clocking in 7-9 hours each night. A well-rested individual can face the day's challenges with resilience and clarity.

Understanding the Importance of Sleep: Sleep, often taken for granted, serves as a cornerstone for our holistic well-being. Its transformative effects span from the cognitive realms to the very fibers of our physical constitution.

Optimal Brain Function: During the deep stages of sleep, our brain actively consolidates memories, processes the day's information, and prepares for the upcoming challenges. This ensures we wake up with a refreshed mind, ready for critical thinking, problem-solving, and innovation.

Emotional Balance: Adequate rest acts as an emotional stabilizer. The REM (Rapid Eye Movement) phase of sleep is particularly vital for emotional and mental health. It aids in processing emotional experiences, potentially reducing the risk of mental health disorders like depression and anxiety.

Physical Stamina: Beyond the mind, sleep plays a pivotal role in bodily repair and rejuvenation. As we sleep, our bodies actively repair damaged cells, rejuvenate the cardiovascular system, and optimize energy reserves, ensuring we're physically equipped to tackle the next day.

Implementing Healthy Sleep Practices: Understanding the importance of sleep is one thing; ensuring we get quality rest is another. Here's how to create an environment conducive to rejuvenating sleep:

Consistent Sleep Schedule: Just as we set routines for work or exercise, sleep too thrives on consistency. Endeavor to go to bed and wake up at the same time daily, even on weekends. This regularity reinforces the body's natural circadian rhythm, making falling asleep and waking up more effortless over time.

Optimal Sleep Duration: While the general recommendation hovers around 7-9 hours for adults, it's crucial to listen to your body. Some might feel fully refreshed with seven hours, while others might need a full nine. Track your sleep and adjust based on when you feel most alert and vibrant.

Crafting the Right Environment: Your bedroom should be a sanctuary optimized for rest. Consider investing in a comfortable mattress and pillows. Ensure the room is dark, quiet, and cool. Eliminating electronic distractions and minimizing noise can further enhance sleep quality.

Pre-Sleep Rituals: The activities leading up to bedtime can significantly impact our sleep quality. Consider incorporating calming practices such as reading, taking a warm bath, or practicing deep breathing exercises. Avoid caffeine or heavy meals before bedtime, as they can disrupt sleep.

Exhausted
BK via NightCafe AI

In essence, sleep is not just a mere act of shutting our eyes. It's a potent tool in our arsenal, paving the way for enhanced productivity, emotional stability, and physical vitality. By prioritizing rest and optimizing our sleep practices, we equip ourselves with the resilience and clarity needed to navigate life's myriad challenges. Remember, in the journey of balancing health and wealth, sleep can indeed be our most valuable ally.

2. Dental Health - A Window to Overall Health:
Why: Routine dental care and checkups curb the onset of potential dental complications, which can be financially draining.
How: Daily oral hygiene practices combined with bi-annual check-ups can preempt costly treatments.
The Interconnectedness of Oral and Overall Well-being: While

our teeth may be a small part of our body, they can tell a grand story about our overall health. Dental health isn't just about a gleaming smile or avoiding cavities; it's intricately connected to, and can significantly influence, the broader spectrum of our well-being.

Significance of Oral Health: Dental issues can be indicative of deeper underlying health conditions. For instance, gum infections have been linked to heart diseases, diabetes, and even complications during pregnancy. What begins in the mouth can quickly permeate other systems, showcasing the interconnectedness of our body's functions.

Financial Implications: Dental emergencies, when neglected, can lead to treatments that are not only physically taxing but also come with hefty price tags. Whether it's a root canal, crown, or extraction, the costs can escalate quickly, making preventative care a wise financial decision.

Taking Proactive Measures for Dental Health: Understanding the importance of oral health paves the way for implementing effective preventative measures.

Daily Oral Hygiene: This is the frontline defense against most dental issues. Brushing your teeth at least twice a day with fluoride toothpaste, followed by flossing, ensures the removal of food particles and bacteria. Using a mouthwash can further reduce bacteria that cause plaque and gum disease.

Bi-annual Dental Check-ups: Regular visits to the dentist, typically every six months, are crucial. These check-ups allow for professional cleanings to remove hardened plaque, assessment of potential problem areas, and early detection of issues like cavities or gum diseases. Early interventions can prevent complicated procedures and thus reduce associated costs.

Dietary Choices: What we consume has a direct impact on our dental health. Reducing sugary snacks and beverages can lower the risk of cavities. Consuming a balanced diet rich in calcium and vitamin D supports strong teeth and gums.

Avoiding Tobacco: Smoking or chewing tobacco can increase the risk of gum disease and oral cancer. Steering clear of tobacco products can significantly enhance oral health and reduce associated treatment costs.

Protective Measures: For those engaged in contact sports or activities, using mouthguards can prevent dental injuries. Similarly, if you're prone to grinding your teeth at night, consider a protective night guard.

Prioritizing the prevention of gum disease is crucial, given its status as the primary cause of tooth loss. Dentists often recommend brushing the gums as well as the teeth, yet unfortunately, gums are often overlooked due to a lack of patient knowledge. This serves as a cautionary note about potential consequences in old age, such as dealing with ill-fitting dentures. Emphasizing dental care underscores the enduring benefits of such investments in your long-term health.

In conclusion, our mouths serve as gateways to our overall health and financial well-being. Recognizing the profound impact of oral health and taking proactive measures ensures a healthy life and the potential to save thousands in unforeseen medical expenses. Every time you pick up that toothbrush or schedule a dental check-up, you're making an investment not only in your oral health but also in your broader physical and financial well-being.

3. Nutrition - Fueling the Body Right:

Basics: The focus should be on nutrient-dense foods, encompassing fresh vegetables, lean meats, and grains.

Drinks: Swap the sugary beverages for water, herbal teas, or infused drinks.

Budget-Friendly Healthy Choices: Explore local farmers' markets, participate in community gardening, or start a small kitchen garden. These not only reduce expenses but also ensure you're consuming fresh and uncontaminated produce.

Understanding the Significance of Nutrition: Before diving into the details, it's crucial to understand why nutrition is paramount. Our bodies operate similarly to machines, where the quality of fuel determines performance. Good nutrition isn't just about staying fit or losing weight; it's about enhancing the body's functions, boosting mental clarity, and reducing the risk of chronic diseases, which can lead to hefty medical bills. It's an investment in health today that can save money in the future.

Embracing Nutrient-dense Foods: Nourishing the Body with Basics: Your daily meals should be packed with nutrient-rich foods that offer maximum health benefits per calorie consumed. This includes:

Fresh Vegetables: Dark leafy greens like kale and spinach, cruciferous veggies like broccoli and cauliflower, and colorful options like bell peppers and carrots are powerhouses of vitamins, minerals, and antioxidants.

Lean Meats: Chicken, turkey, and fish provide the necessary protein without the saturated fats often found in red meats. They're essential for muscle building and repairing bodily tissues.

Whole Grains: Foods like quinoa, brown rice, and oats are excellent sources of dietary fiber and essential nutrients, promoting better digestion and sustained energy throughout the day.

Rethinking Your Beverage Choices: The Fluid Shift: Our bodies are predominantly water, making fluid intake vital. However, not all drinks benefit our health.

Water: The ultimate elixir of life, water flushes out toxins, aids digestion, and hydrates the body. Ensure you're consuming enough daily.

Herbal Teas: Options like green tea, chamomile, and peppermint not only hydrate but also offer a range of health benefits, from antioxidants to calming properties.

Infused Drinks: Add a zing to your regular water by infusing it with natural flavors from fruits, cucumbers, or herbs. This way, you're adding subtle flavors without the sugars found in commercial drinks.

Affordable Nutritional Choices - Good Health Doesn't Need to

Break the Bank:

For many, the notion of healthy eating often seems synonymous with expensive. But with a little creativity and effort, it's possible to nourish your body without straining your wallet.

Local Farmers' Markets: These can be treasure troves of fresh, locally grown produce, often priced lower than big supermarkets. Additionally, you're supporting local farmers, which is a win-win!

Community Gardening: Engaging in community gardens allows you access to fresh produce while also building a sense of community. It's a hands-on way to understand where your food comes from.

Kitchen Gardens: Starting a small garden at home, even if it's just a few pots of herbs on a balcony, can drastically reduce costs. Plus, there's a unique satisfaction in consuming something you've grown yourself.

In conclusion, making mindful nutritional choices isn't just a pathway to better health; it's a strategic approach to financial wellness. With every healthy meal or drink, you're taking a step towards disease prevention and, in the long run, potential savings on medical expenses. Nutrition isn't just about food; it's about future-proofing your body and bank account.

4. Fitness - Wealth in Movement:

Free Fitness: Engage in no-cost activities like walking, using stairs, or following online fitness tutorials.

The Routine: Incorporate at least 20 minutes of active movement daily. Consistent physical activity wards off various ailments, leading to reduced medical expenses.

Understanding the Interconnection of Fitness and Finances: At the nexus of physical health and financial stability lies an often overlooked truth: investing time and energy into fitness can translate into tangible monetary savings. The adage "health is wealth" isn't just metaphorical; staying fit can substantially reduce medical bills, enhance productivity, and improve overall quality of life, which can indirectly influence earning potential.

Exploring Cost-free Fitness Ventures: In a world that often associates fitness with expensive gym memberships or high-end equipment, it's essential to debunk the myth that fitness needs to be pricey.

Walking: One of the simplest yet most effective forms of exercise. Whether it's a brisk morning walk, a stroll through a local park, or just choosing to walk short distances instead of driving, every step contributes to cardiovascular health and calorie burn.

Using Stairs: Elevators and escalators might be convenient, but stairs offer a quick cardiovascular and strength-building workout. Regularly choosing stairs can tone the legs and boost stamina.

Online Fitness Tutorials: The digital age is a boon for fitness enthusiasts. From YouTube to various fitness apps, there's an abundance of high-quality workout tutorials available for free. Whether you're into aerobics, yoga, HIIT, or dance workouts, there's something for everyone.

Establishing a Daily Fitness Routine: While sporadic workouts are beneficial, consistency is the key to lasting health benefits.

Setting Aside Time: Dedicate at least 20 minutes daily to physical activity. This doesn't mean intense workouts every day; even light stretching or a short walk counts.

Variety is the Spice of Fitness: Change up your routine to keep things exciting and ensure a well-rounded workout. For instance, if you did cardio exercises one day, focus on strength training or flexibility the next.

Monitoring Progress: Track your activities, set small goals, and celebrate when you achieve them. It can be as simple as walking an extra 500 steps or holding a plank for a few seconds longer. Progress, no matter how small, is motivating.

The Long-term Financial Benefits: Engaging in regular physical activity has an array of health benefits, including reduced risk of chronic diseases like heart disease, diabetes, and hypertension. By maintaining good health, you can potentially reduce future medical bills and expenses related to health issues. Additionally, a fit individual is often more energetic, focused, and productive, attributes that can positively influence one's professional life and earnings.

Embarking on a fitness journey isn't just a commitment to physical well-being but also a strategic investment in financial health. By adopting a proactive approach to fitness, the compounded benefits of enhanced health, reduced medical costs, and heightened overall productivity become accessible. In the grand tapestry of life, fitness threads weave a resilient fabric of both health and wealth.

5. Sunshine - Nature's Therapy:

Why: Sunlight stimulates the production of serotonin, elevating mood and mental well-being.

How: Dedicate a few minutes daily to bask in natural sunlight, be it during a morning walk or a short mid-day break.

Unraveling the Science Behind Sunlight: The golden rays of the sun, often symbolized as a source of life and energy, play a pivotal role in our physical and psychological health. Beyond its luminosity, sunlight is a natural elixir that offers a plethora of benefits.

Why Sunlight is Essential: Serotonin Boost: Exposure to sunlight stimulates the brain's production of serotonin, a neurotransmitter responsible for maintaining mood balance. A surge in serotonin levels can alleviate feelings of anxiety and depression, leading to a more positive mindset.

Vitamin D Production: Sunlight is a natural source of Vitamin D, a vital nutrient for bone health, immune system support, and inflammation reduction. In fact, a lack of adequate sunlight can lead to Vitamin D deficiency, which has been linked to various health complications.

Regulation of Sleep-Wake Cycle: Sunlight also influences the production of melatonin, a hormone that regulates sleep. By aligning our body's internal clock, or circadian rhythm, exposure to natural light during the day can improve sleep quality at night.

Basking in the Sun
BK via Night Cafe AI

How to Harness the Benefits of Sunshine:

Morning Rituals: Start your day by stepping outside and soaking in the morning sun. Whether it's a quick stretch on your patio, a jog around the block, or simply sipping your coffee by the window, these moments can set a positive tone for the day.

Short Breaks: Incorporate short sunlight breaks into your routine. If you're working indoors, take a few minutes every couple of hours to step outside. This not only gives you a dose of sunlight but also provides a mental break, boosting productivity.

Mindful Sunbathing: Choose a comfortable spot, maybe in your garden or a nearby park, and practice mindfulness as you bask in the sunlight. Feel the warmth on your skin, listen to the surrounding sounds, and breathe deeply. This meditative practice can amplify the therapeutic effects of sunlight.

Safety First: While sunlight offers numerous benefits, it's crucial to balance exposure to avoid the harmful effects of UV rays. Wearing sunscreen, protective clothing, or sunglasses can safeguard against potential skin damage.

In an age dominated by artificial lights and screen glows, reconnecting with the natural therapy of sunlight is essential. It's a holistic approach to well-being, weaving together the threads of mental peace, physical health, and spiritual rejuvenation. Embrace the sunshine, and let nature's therapy illuminate your path to holistic health.

6. Rethink Sugary Indulgences:

   Why: High sugar intake is a precursor to conditions like diabetes, obesity, and heart ailments.

   How: Gradually phase out sugary products. Satiate sweet cravings with fruits or natural sweeteners, which offer additional nutritional benefits.

   Understanding Sugar and Its Effects: Sugar, while delightful to our taste buds, carries a hidden cost. Its omnipresence in modern diets, often hidden in processed foods, beverages, and even so-called "healthy" snacks, makes it one of the most over-consumed substances today.

   The Sugary Conundrum – Why Limiting is Crucial: The Health Domino Effect: Excessive sugar intake doesn't just affect your waistline. It's a silent instigator of a cascade of health issues. High sugar levels in the bloodstream can lead to insulin resistance, setting the stage for Type 2 diabetes.

Weight Gain Risks: Sugary foods and drinks, especially carbonated beverages, contain high fructose levels, which can lead to increased hunger and promote fat storage in the belly. Over time, this paves the way for obesity.

Heart Health: There's a direct correlation between high sugar consumption and heart diseases. Elevated sugar levels lead to inflammation, high blood triglyceride levels, and high blood pressure – all risk factors for cardiovascular disease.

Tooth Decay: It's no secret that sugar feeds the harmful bacteria in the mouth, leading to cavities and gum disease.

Strategies to Reduce Sugar Intake – The 'How':

Reading Labels: One of the first steps in sugar reduction is awareness. By reading product labels, you can gauge the sugar content, making it easier to opt for lower-sugar or sugar-free alternatives.

Natural Substitutes: When the sweet craving strikes, reach for fruits. Not only do they satisfy the sugar craving, but they also bring a host of vitamins, minerals, and fibers to the table. Natural sweeteners, such as honey, stevia, or maple syrup, can be healthier alternatives to refined sugar.

Limit Sugary Beverages: Soft drinks, fruit juices, and many alcoholic beverages are sugar-laden. Instead, infuse water with slices of fruits, mint, or cucumber for a refreshing, low-calorie drink. Herbal teas, both hot and cold, are also excellent alternatives.

Home-Cooked Meals: Preparing meals at home gives you complete control over the ingredients, making it easier to limit sugar. Plus, there are countless sugar-free recipes available that are both delicious and healthy.

Mindful Desserts: It's possible to enjoy desserts without overindulging in sugar. Many desserts can be made using natural sweeteners or by reducing the sugar quantity. Over time, your palate will adjust, and you'll come to appreciate the subtler, natural sweetness in foods.

Reconfiguring our relationship with sugar is not about deprivation; it's about making conscious choices for a healthier life. By understanding the implications of excessive sugar consumption and taking active steps to reduce it, we pave the way for enhanced well-being, vibrant energy, and a reduced risk of chronic diseases. Embracing a low-sugar lifestyle is an investment in long-term health, ensuring that the sweetness of life is derived from moments, memories, and experiences, rather than fleeting sugary indulgences.

7. In the complex realm of tobacco and smoking, it's essential to start by emphasizing the gravity of this habit. While the initial allure may be the rush and appetite suppression that tobacco offers, it's crucial to understand that these fleeting benefits are vastly outweighed by the long-term harm they pose to your health and financial stability.

Every inhalation of smoke, taken with any degree of regularity, is an investment in future medical bills and a potential threat to your overall well-being. The costs of a tobacco addiction, and indeed any form of addiction, can be astronomical, rapidly eroding your savings and jeopardizing your future prospects. In simple terms, the wisest course of action is to never embark on this journey. Starting smoking is a decision that comes with profound and lasting consequences, making it a path best left untraveled. If you engage in regular or excessive smoking or drinking, you have already given up.

In conclusion, marrying the principles of health and wealth doesn't have to be an arduous task. Every conscious decision geared towards health can have ripple effects, enhancing financial stability. As these incremental changes compound, the distant dream of a harmonious balance between health and financial freedom becomes an achievable, tangible reality. Remember, it's the small, daily choices that pave the road to a life of abundance.

Did I mention cut back on sugary drinks enough?

When grappling with a medical issue, the unfortunate reality often demands that you delve into your own research. My upbringing in Mississippi exposed me to a significant variance in the competency levels of medical professionals. The journey commenced in high school when I began experiencing issues with food intermittently getting stuck in my throat. This concern prompted visits to numerous doctors and clinics across three different states over the years. It wasn't until 14 years later, armed with good health insurance, that I found myself under the care of a specialist in Jackson, MS—the state capital. This ENT (ear, nose, throat) doctor adeptly identified the problem and swiftly rectified it in less than a week. Utilizing a throat scope, he pinpointed a ring of scar tissue resulting from acid reflux. The solution was elegantly simple—using a balloon to break the scar tissue—and prescribing omeprazole. Fourteen years of suffering, remedied in a week. The lesson here is crystal clear: when seeking medical assistance, it's vital to enter your appointments armed with information about your condition. A key detail in your description might spark insights for diagnosis and treatment in the doctor's mind. If your healthcare provider doesn't immediately offer solutions, don't hesitate to propose tests and potential causes. In certain instances, seeking second opinions or, in extreme situations, finding a new doctor may be imperative to ensure thorough and effective care.

4

Home and Auto Maintenance

Home ownership, or even renting, is both a privilege and a responsibility. The ongoing care of your home not only ensures its aesthetic and functional appeal but can prevent minor issues from snowballing into major expenses. This chapter aims to guide homeowners through a basic year-round maintenance schedule. For renters, you should first try to get your landlord to have some of the more intensive, or expensive, items done for you, but basic home maintenance is still your responsibility.

Year-Round Maintenance Checklist:

- Inspect and Maintain HVAC System:
    - Why: For optimal performance and increased longevity.

- ○ How: Hire a professional for a comprehensive check. Also, replace or clean filters regularly.
- ○ Frequency: Service annually; replace filters every 6 months.
- Inspect Water Heater and HVAC Drain Pans:
  - ○ Why: Overflow or leaks can cause damage.
  - ○ How: Look for signs of rust, leakage, or overflow.
  - ○ Frequency: Every 6 months.
- Inspect and Clean Gutters:
  - ○ Why: Debris-clogged gutters can lead to water damage, pests, and foundation issues.
  - ○ How: Use a ladder to safely reach the gutters, remove debris by hand, and rinse with a hose.
  - ○ Frequency: At least twice a year, in spring and fall.
- Check for Window and Door Leaks:
  - ○ Why: Drafts increase energy bills and can make indoor living less comfortable.
  - ○ How: Hold a lit incense stick near all window and door edges. If smoke blows sideways, you have a draft. Seal leaks with   weatherstripping or caulk.
  - ○ Frequency: Annually.
- Test Smoke and Carbon Monoxide Detectors:
  - ○ Why: They're vital for safety.
  - ○ How: Press the "test" button on each device.
  - ○ Frequency: Test monthly; replace batteries annually.
- Check Water Filters in Refrigerators:
  - ○ Why: To ensure efficiency and food safety.
  - ○ How: Refer to your refrigerator's manual for the location and cleaning/replacement instructions.

- Frequency: Every 6 months.
- Dryer Vent Cleaning:
    - Why: Lint buildup can lead to decreased efficiency or fires.
    - How: Disconnect the dryer vent and vacuum out lint, or hire a professional.
    - Frequency: Annually.
- Clean Garbage Disposal:
    - Why: Prevent clogs and odors.
    - How: Run cold water, add a cup of ice and a half cup of salt, then turn on the disposal. After grinding, add lemon peels for freshness.
    - Frequency: Every 6 months.
- Check Sump Pumps (if applicable):
    - Why: Prevent basement flooding.
    - How: Pour a bucket of water into the sump pit. The pump should activate, remove the water, and turn off seamlessly.
    - Frequency: Annually.
- Inspect Water Softener:
    - Why: Ensure effective water softening.
    - How: Check for salt bridge formations and maintain salt levels.
    - Frequency: Every 4 months.

Seasonal Maintenance:

Spring:

- Check the Exterior:

- ○ Why: Winter can cause a myriad of damages.
- ○ How: Walk around your home, noting any peeling paint, damaged siding, or compromised roofing.
- ○ Frequency: At the beginning of the season.
- Service the Air Conditioning System:
  - ○ Why: Ensure it's prepared for the summer.
  - ○ How: Hire a professional for thorough servicing.
  - ○ Frequency: Annually.

Summer:

- Trim Trees and Shrubs:
  - ○ Why: Prevent damage or pest access.
  - ○ How: Use pruning shears for small branches or hire a professional for larger trees.
  - ○ Frequency: At the start of the season.
- Outdoor Spaces Maintenance:
  - ○ Why: Extend their lifespan.
  - ○ How: Clean furniture, reseal wooden decks, and check patios for cracks.
  - ○ Frequency: Twice during the season.

Autumn:

- Chimney and Fireplace Cleaning:
  - ○ Why: Soot buildup is flammable.
  - ○ How: Hire a professional chimney sweep.
  - ○ Frequency: Before the first use each season.
- Roof and Gutters:

- ○ Why: Prevent water damage.
- ○ How: Inspect visually; hire a professional for any repairs.
- ○ Frequency: At the end of the fall season.

Winter:

- Insulate Pipes:
    - ○ Why: Prevent freezing and bursting.
    - ○ How: Use foam pipe insulators.
    - ○ Frequency: Before the first freeze.
- Seal Windows and Doors:
    - ○ Why: Retain indoor heat.
    - ○ How: Apply weatherstripping or window film where needed.
    - ○ Frequency: At the start of the season.

Beyond the bricks and mortar of a house lie responsibilities that encompass the entirety of our surroundings. Yard maintenance, for those fortunate to have one, becomes a pivotal aspect of homeownership. Trees and bushes need trimming to ensure they don't become hazards or breeding grounds for pests. Drainage systems around the property should be routinely checked and cleaned to prevent flooding and water damage.

The comprehensive care of our abode doesn't end at its four walls. It extends to every nook and cranny, every green patch, and every water flow channel that surrounds it.

Consistent maintenance, though often neglected, is crucial for retaining your home's worth and averting expensive repairs.

By dedicating time and occasionally a modest investment early on, both homeowners and renters can achieve substantial savings and lasting peace of mind. The cornerstone of a pristine and inviting home lies in regular inspections and proactive measures. If ever in doubt, the internet is a treasure trove of resources, and many professionals offer affordable inspections, providing valuable advice and carrying out necessary repairs.

Just as homes need regular upkeep, vehicles demand routine attention. Regular vehicle maintenance not only ensures safe driving but also prolongs the life of the car, resulting in potential cost savings in the long term. In this section, we'll dive into essential maintenance practices to keep your vehicle in peak condition.

Essential Maintenance Checklist:

- Oil Change:
    - Why: Clean oil lubricates the engine, reduces friction, and prevents overheating.
    - How: Refer to the vehicle manual for the recommended oil type and change frequency. Either change it yourself or have it done at a service center.
    - Frequency: Typically, every 3,000 to 5,000 miles, but modern cars may vary.
- Rotate and Check Tires:
    - Why: Even tire wear ensures a smoother ride and longer tire life.

- How: Change the position of the tires according to manufacturer's recommendation. Also, check for tire tread depth to ensure safety.
  - Frequency: Every 6,000 to 8,000 miles or as advised in the manual.
- Air Filter Replacement:
  - Why: A clean air filter enhances engine efficiency and performance.
  - How: Remove the old filter and replace it with a new one. The process is straightforward in most vehicles.
  - Frequency: Annually or every 12,000 miles, whichever comes first.
- Cabin Air Filter Change:
  - Why: Ensure fresh air inside the cabin and improve AC performance.
  - How: Locate the filter (usually behind the glove box), remove and replace. Some models might require more intricate steps.
  - Frequency: Every 15,000 to 30,000 miles or as recommended.
- Brake Check:
  - Why: Ensure safety and optimal stopping power.
  - How: Listen for screeches when braking; it's an indicator of wear. A professional should inspect the brake system periodically.
  - Frequency: At least once a year.
- Coolant Check:

- ○ Why: Prevents the engine from overheating or freezing.
- ○ How: Check the coolant reservoir's level and refill if low with a mix of water and antifreeze.
- ○ Frequency: Before summer and winter, and any time the level looks low.
- Battery Maintenance:
  - ○ Why: Ensure reliable starts and vehicle operation.
  - ○ How: Check battery terminals for corrosion. Clean using a solution of baking soda and water.
  - ○ Frequency: Every 6 months.
- Wiper Blades Replacement:
  - ○ Why: Ensures clear visibility during rain.
  - ○ How: Slide off old blades and attach new ones. It's a quick DIY task.
  - ○ Frequency: Annually or when streaking starts.

Maintaining your vehicle is more than a chore; it's an investment. By addressing minor issues promptly and sticking to a regular maintenance schedule, you can avoid many potential costly repairs and extend the lifespan of your vehicle. Just as with home maintenance, the key is consistency. By attending to both your home and vehicle with care and regularity, you ensure that they serve you reliably, safely, and efficiently for years to come.

5

Managing Debt and Savings

I know, a book on escaping poverty waits until chapter 5 to cover Money, Debt and Savings? Yes. It is more important to acquire the tools to make a living, keep more of the money you earn and then manage that money wisely. To that end, lets discuss debt and savings a little further!

The financial landscape often appears skewed toward benefiting institutions rather than individuals. In this challenging environment, it's crucial to align with entities genuinely committed to your financial well-being. Simultaneously, awareness of financial traps and roadblocks prevalent in the modern financial world is essential.

In finance, it's vital to recognize that only specific financial advisors, such as certified financial planners and registered investment advisors, are bound by fiduciary duties. These professionals prioritize your interests over potential profits for themselves. On the contrary, entities like banks, credit card companies, and loan originators lack such obligations. Their primary duty is to produce maximum profits for their shareholders, not necessarily ensuring your financial well-being.

Shareholder Profits
BK via Night Cafe AI

Navigating through this financial landscape requires caution and awareness of potential pitfalls. Overdraft fees, late charges, and high credit card interest rates, especially for those with modest resources, can be insidious. Traditional banks, more often than not, offer less favorable deals to individuals with limited funds, reinforcing the notion that substantial assets are a prerequisite for favorable treatment.

Keep in mind that conventional financial institutions, especially those lacking a fiduciary obligation, may not prioritize individuals with modest assets. However, the evolution of finance has given rise to alternative establishments like credit unions, which frequently provide more favorable terms for modest savers. Additionally, modern financial tools, ranging from budgeting apps to credit monitors, offer actionable insights, making financial health more accessible.

Exercise caution when dealing with companies that promise quick financial fixes. Businesses offering services like Rent-To-Own, Title Loans, or Payday Loans might seem appealing initially, but they often conceal hidden issues that lead to more debt. Amid these challenges, prioritize connecting with partners, especially those with a legal duty (fiduciaries), who genuinely support your financial well-being and growth.

Cultivating a Saving Ethic:

Start Modestly: Even if it's just a small portion of your paycheck, prioritize saving it routinely. The primary goal initially is to nurture the discipline of saving, not necessarily the quantity.

Scale Up Gradually: As your financial inflows increase, incrementally elevate your savings percentage - you should aim for saving 30% of your income. Challenge yourself annually, or even monthly, to see if you can allocate a bit more towards savings without compromising your daily needs. Starting to save early can lead to a much better retirement. A good savings plan started at 21 can help you retire in only 29 years and enjoy life for a while. (more on this later in the chapter)

Establish a Robust Safety Net:

Assess Your Monthly Expenditures: Carefully itemize every recurring expense you incur, from essentials like housing and food to discretionary items like entertainment. Make sure that you can cover these expenses at the right time each time they come up, whether monthly, quarterly or annually.

Forge a Financial Buffer: Endeavor to amass a minimum of two months' worth of these outgoings in an interest bearing savings account. This reservoir will become indispensable during unforeseen financial disruptions, be it medical emergencies, sudden layoffs, or unexpected home repairs.

Navigating the savings journey isn't always a straightforward path. As I pen this in 2023, reflecting on my own journey from 2004, I acknowledge the trials of building that savings nest. If only I had embraced the savings discipline earlier, perhaps I'd be relishing the pleasures of retirement right now, fulfilling my dreams of globetrotting. Sadly, I'm still in pursuit of stashing away that foundational two months of expenses in an accessible savings account. Additionally, I'm striving to bolster my retirement funds to ensure a future where I'm not grappling with financial constraints. And, adding to the problems that have built up, I still struggle with using my credit cards wisely. My aspiration is that this book equips you with the wisdom to carve a better financial path, allowing you to embrace the joys of an early retirement and a life filled with enriching experiences.

Find a Suitable Financial Partner:

Credit Union Advantage: Compared to mainstream banks, credit unions frequently present superior interest yields and fewer fees, thereby enhancing your savings growth rate.

Within my credit union, I've strategically structured my accounts to maximize benefits. Firstly, there's the Membership Account that holds the equivalent of one full paycheck. Though it earns a modest interest, it's my foundational layer. Secondly, I leverage the Credit Union's High-Interest Checking Account, which offers a notably competitive rate. Here, I safeguard the equivalent of two months of expenses, and whenever possible, a little more. Lastly, I operate a separate Checking Account dedicated to managing monthly bills. After payday, it experiences a brief influx, but as next payday approaches, the balance usually hovers around a minimal sum. A safety net woven into this arrangement is the automatic overdraft protection from the Membership Account. This prevents any overdraft fees, provided it's not overutilized.

Embrace FinTech:

Modern apps, such as Acorns, can automate your savings by rounding up purchases and funneling the change into investments. It's a painless and effective way to bolster your savings without even noticing it.

I've incorporated financial technology into my financial strategy by utilizing Acorns. Specifically, I allocate the 20% of my income designated for Mental Wellness to an Acorns checking account. This is where I draw funds from, using its debit card, for incidental expenses like lunches, gas, snacks, and other discretionary activities not classified as regular bills. Alongside this, I actively contribute to both Acorns Invest and Acorns Later accounts. The Invest account serves as a savings buffer, which, while accessible, is not immediately liquid. It boasts a commendable year-over-year return, making it a rewarding savings vessel. On the other hand, the Later account is a tax-advantaged IRA. This structure translates to tax savings, evident when I notice a heftier tax refund after filing.

Oversee Your Financial Health:

Embrace Financial Dashboards: Platforms like Mint provide an encompassing view of your finances, highlighting patterns, helping rein in unnecessary expenditures, and facilitating informed budgeting. Many contemporary banks and credit unions offer analogous features; my credit union aptly labels it "Link External Accounts," allowing visibility into balances and transactions of connected accounts. However, given the heightened security measures and multi-factor authentication nowadays, some accounts may not seamlessly integrate. Thus, periodic manual checks on individual financial sites are essential to maintain a holistic grasp of your monetary well-being.

Monitor Your Credit Health: Utilize platforms like Credit Karma to stay informed about your credit score and gain valuable insights into its improvement. This becomes particularly crucial when you're in pursuit of favorable loan conditions or navigating housing arrangements. In the complex world of personal finance, comprehending credit scores is indispensable. Although this book doesn't delve into the intricate details due to scope limitations, understanding the essence of credit scores—how they're calculated and their diverse applications—remains essential for informed financial decision-making.

Quick Tips for Building and Enhancing Your Credit Score:

* Timely Bill Payments Matter: Ensure all your bills are paid promptly.

* Explore Secured Credit Options: Consider obtaining a Secured Credit Card or applying for a Credit-builder Loan.

* Leverage Authorized User Status: Enhance your credit profile by becoming an authorized user on a credit account.

* Seek Credit Limit Upgrades: Request an increase in your credit limit to positively impact your credit score.

Strategic Investments:

Once your initial savings targets are achieved and you have surplus from the 30% Finances portion of your income, consider stepping into the investment realm. Before diving in, spend time on self-education or seek advice from trusted financial consultants. The primary goal is to judiciously grow your wealth, rather than gamble it away.

For those who might be unfamiliar, a fiduciary is an individual or organization that manages money and has a legal obligation to act in another's best financial interests. They hold a bond of trust with clients, ensuring transparency and avoiding conflicts of interest. Fiduciary responsibilities span various professional domains. Board members, for instance, often owe fiduciary duties to their organizations. Trustees similarly owe fiduciary responsibilities to their beneficiaries. In the corporate arena, retirement plan administrators typically bear fiduciary duties to their company's workforce.

Diversification is more than just a financial catchphrase; it's a proven approach. Spread your investments across various assets such as stocks, bonds, real estate, or burgeoning industries. This tactic not only dilutes risk but also positions you to benefit from varied market trends. Additionally, explore options like annuities, Certificates of Deposit (CDs), and consider amplifying your contributions to employer-sponsored or individual retirement plans.

Charting a Long-Term Financial Course:

Leverage Employer-Sponsored Retirement plans: If your employer offers a 401(k) or similar retirement plan, especially with matched contributions, it's imperative to maximize your participation. Think of it as a double win: not only are you saving for your golden years, but you're effectively receiving 'bonus' funds from your employer in the process.

Planning for retirement involves a degree of subjectivity, requiring estimations of future living expenses, anticipated interest rates, and determining the necessary savings to meet financial goals. For example, initiating retirement savings with an initial deposit of $100 in an account offering a 5% Annual Percentage Yield (APY) and consistently contributing $1,965 per month over 29 years could accumulate $1,503,362. This sum has the potential to generate $75,000 per year in interest, forming a substantial foundation for retirement income. While the idea of contributing almost $2,000 per month may see daunting, that is assuming a 5% APY, and I have investments that are getting higher returns over the long term - one at 6.32%, another getting 17%, and one currently sitting at a measly 2.3%. It's evident that relying solely on a simple savings account is unlikely to lead to the desired financial security. You need a solid plan, tailored to your needs and income - which means research, careful selection of investments and, maybe, some planning assistance.

In today's volatile financial landscape, possessing a strategic blueprint for managing debt and savings isn't just savvy—it's indispensable. Such a roadmap not only ensures you navigate the ebb and flow of economic challenges but also primes you for a future replete with financial security and peace. Remember, with every conscientious financial decision today, you're sowing the seeds for a more prosperous tomorrow.

6

Invest in Quality

"The reason that the rich were so rich, Vimes reasoned, was because they managed to spend less money.

Take boots, for example. He earned thirty-eight dollars a month plus allowances. A really good pair of leather boots cost fifty dollars. But an affordable pair of boots, which were sort of OK for a season or two and then leaked like hell when the cardboard gave out, cost about ten dollars. Those were the kind of boots Vimes always bought, and wore until the soles were so thin that he could tell where he was in Ankh-Morpork on a foggy night by the feel of the cobbles.

But the thing was that good boots lasted for years and years. A man who could afford fifty dollars had a pair of boots that'd still be keeping his feet dry in ten years' time, while the poor man who could only afford cheap boots would have spent a hundred dollars on boots in the same time and would still have wet feet."

Men at Arms, Terry Pratchett

The Cost of Poverty

The idea that poverty comes with a high price might sound surprising, but the everyday reality for those stuck in its grip sheds light on this truth. Living in poverty often means relying on low-cost, short-term solutions, which, in the long run, turn out to be more expensive both financially and emotionally. Purchasing something only to see it break or wear out quickly can feel like a personal setback or just another obstacle keeping you down. Essentially, poverty pushes individuals into an ongoing cycle of makeshift solutions, where inexpensive items break down faster, leading to frequent replacements or repairs.

The Never-Ending Loop

Consider purchasing cheap shoes that wear out quickly, prompting you to buy new ones frequently. In a year, the overall cost may surpass what you would have spent on one durable pair initially. Now, expand this concept to everything you need, such as appliances and clothes. The costs of consistently choosing these "budget-friendly" options start accumulating over time.

Good Boots
BK via Night Cafe AI

However, when decisions are based on the immediate availability of funds, considering long-term value becomes challenging. Yet, the constant cycle of replacing or repairing items not only drains finances but also consumes time and emotional energy.

The Value in Quality

To escape the cycle of frequent replacements and repairs, the goal is to gradually shift toward prioritizing quality and durability over mere affordability. Quality items often boast extended lifespans, superior performance, and, in some cases, warranties protecting against premature malfunctions.

Take kitchen appliances, for example. While a quality blender may require a higher upfront cost, its durability justifies the investment, outlasting cheaper alternatives that need annual replacements or repairs. Similarly, investing in a well-made coat, though it may seem like a splurge, provides far more value than purchasing multiple cheaper ones over the same timeframe, as it offers lasting warmth while withstanding daily wear and tear.

Unfortunately, consumer behavior significantly contributes to the prevalence of built-in obsolescence. Studies indicate that consumers often prioritize new, innovative products over durable ones, influenced by factors like the desire for the latest technology and the psychological satisfaction derived from acquiring something new.

From a business standpoint, the economic model of planned obsolescence offers distinct advantages. Manufacturers intentionally design products with limited lifespans, encouraging frequent replacements or upgrades, stimulating economic activity, and fostering industry growth.

In highly competitive markets, companies face pressure to release new products and stay ahead of rivals, emphasizing innovation and frequent releases over the longevity of goods. Businesses may find it challenging to thrive if they do not align with the rapid pace of product turnover characterizing many industries.

Producing highly durable items often involves premium materials and advanced technologies, leading to higher production costs. While quality products attract a niche market willing to pay a premium, the broader consumer base often prioritizes affordability over longevity. This cost-conscious mindset contributes to the prevalence of products with built-in obsolescence.

A consequence of the built-in obsolescence model is an increase in electronic waste and environmental degradation. The continuous disposal of products with artificially shortened lifespans contributes to pollution and resource depletion. Efforts to mitigate these impacts involve advocating for sustainable and durable product design, with some regions considering regulations to address the issue.

In summary, the prevalence of built-in obsolescence is deeply intertwined with consumer behavior, economic incentives, market competition, cost considerations, environmental impact, and regulatory measures. While awareness of the downsides is growing, changing the existing business model requires a shift in both consumer preferences and industry practices.

House Maintenance and Repairs: Investing in Professionalism

A crucial aspect often overlooked in the cycle of makeshift solutions is home maintenance and repairs. For individuals living in poverty, the temptation to rig something temporarily to save costs is understandable. However, relying on makeshift solutions can lead to more significant issues down the line and end up being more expensive in the long run.

When it comes to maintaining your home, especially for repairs requiring professional expertise, cutting corners may not be the wisest approach. Hiring professionals ensures that the job is done correctly, reducing the likelihood of recurring problems and the need for frequent repairs. While the upfront cost of professional services may seem daunting, it often pales in comparison to the cumulative expenses of repeatedly fixing temporary solutions.

There may be a temptation to have friends or acquaintances do the work. However, it's crucial to recognize the potential risks inherent in this approach. Entrusting critical repairs to individuals without professional credentials may lead to sub-par work, and in more severe cases, could result in significant complications. Attempting to seek compensation from a friend in such circumstances can strain relationships and lead to un-desirable consequences.

Opting for professional services brings a level of assurance and legal protection. Reputable professionals are, or should be, licensed, bonded, and insured. This not only signifies their ex-pertise but also provides you with a legal recourse in case their work falls below the expected standards. Choosing professionals for your home repairs ensures accountability, quality assurance, and peace of mind, safeguarding you from potential headaches and fostering a sense of trust in the maintenance of your living space.

The Journey Out of Poverty:

Escaping the clutches of poverty is undeniably challenging, replete with pitfalls and hard choices. However, by gradually shifting one's mindset from immediate affordability to long-term value, the path becomes clearer. It's about recognizing that sometimes, investing in a slightly more expensive product today leads to savings tomorrow. As one progresses on this path, seeking financial partners and tools that genuinely advocate for their interests becomes crucial. The goal isn't just to escape poverty but to build a foundation for lasting financial security and prosperity.

7

The Education Barrier

A Stark Reality Check:

The age-old adage "Pull yourself up by your bootstraps and get an education" paints a simplified and often unrealistic picture of the educational landscape. It implies that education—a universally acknowledged ladder to success—is accessible to all, overlooking glaring disparities.

A child in an affluent neighborhood might attend a school furnished with the latest tech, diverse extracurriculars, and highly qualified educators. In stark contrast, a child from an impoverished background might struggle with not just inadequate educational tools but basic necessities. Hunger, for instance, can be a formidable barrier. A young mind distracted by an empty stomach or a tumultuous home environment finds it challenging to concentrate, further widening the educational chasm.

This disparity extends to the curriculum too. Take comprehensive sex education—a topic not just about reproduction but about understanding one's body, consent, boundaries, and relationships. Yet, many institutions, especially those in under-privileged regions, offer a watered-down version or skip it altogether, leaving students ill-equipped to navigate life's complexities.

Moreover, as if these challenges weren't enough, there's growing concern over political strategies that could further exacerbate educational disparities. Initiatives like voucher programs, although presented as means to enhance educational choice, often siphon off essential funds from already struggling public schools, further undermining their ability to provide quality education.

A Curriculum for Life:

Education transcends the boundaries of academic proficiency; it is the cornerstone for nurturing individuals equipped to navigate the complexities of the real world. In countless underserved communities, educational institutions grapple with a scarcity of resources. These aren't merely schools with tattered textbooks or missing chalkboards; they're places where passionate educators are stretched thin, managing oversized classes, and where extracurriculars—crucial for holistic development—are deemed luxuries. Chronic underfunding affects not just infrastructure but the caliber of education imparted, creating environments less conducive to nurturing young minds.

In designing our curricula, we must transcend conventional boundaries and incorporate lessons that extend beyond textbooks. Much like the transformative insights shared in this book, these lessons should be seamlessly woven into standard education, recognizing that some parents or guardians may face challenges in providing such guidance at home. Early intervention becomes paramount, acting as a preventative measure to steer our youth away from perilous paths. The curriculum should extend beyond traditional subjects, encompassing essential life skills. Mental health education, strategies for coping with stress, navigating disappointment, and channeling anger constructively should be integral components. By fostering a holistic approach to education, we not only impart knowledge but empower the next generation with the resilience and skills necessary for a thriving future.

After School Education:

In our current era, the responsibility for our ongoing financial and social education lies in our hands, with a vast array of resources available on the internet. Navigating this digital landscape requires the development of discernment skills to differentiate between propaganda, scams, and genuinely valuable insights. Platforms such as The Great Courses, Khan Academy, and Edx.org are viewed as reliable sources for those keen on learning.

The internet, particularly platforms like YouTube, presents an expansive library of educational content. However, within this labyrinth, distinguishing accurate information from misinformation can be a formidable task. I once stumbled upon a well-intentioned video advocating gold as the epitome of "real wealth," a tempting notion that, upon closer examination, revealed complexities related to taxes and coin premiums that could alter its true value. It's essential to recognize that the modern financial landscape no longer ties any country's currency to gold.

To further support your educational journey, I aspire to compile a curated list of links at the conclusion of this work. These links will serve as a regularly updated repository of valuable resources, providing a trustworthy guide for those navigating the intricate world of financial and social education.

Education is Our Future:

In a world brimming with opportunities and challenges alike, education stands as our most potent weapon and our most cherished treasure. If it is to genuinely serve as the master key to prosperity, we must champion it in its most comprehensive form. Beyond just the establishment of schools, it's about sculpting nurturing environments wherein every student, regardless of their initial starting point, is empowered not just to confront the world but to also reimagine and reinvent it.

A future where education is not just a mere formality but a deep, enriching experience, tailored to real-world demands, is a vision we must all rally behind. It's not just an aspirational goal —it's a pressing necessity, an essential commitment to future generations.

And as you turn these pages and glean insights that have the potential to transform lives, remember the power of shared knowledge. If any part of this book has ignited a spark, enriched your understanding, or provided tools for life, consider it your personal mission to pass it on. In a world that can sometimes feel fragmented, it's our collective wisdom, our shared experiences, and our unwavering commitment to lifting each other up, that can make all the difference. Teach, guide, mentor, and inspire—because in the tapestry of human progress, every thread counts.

8

The Other Things

I was taught to shave by Dr. Heathcliff Huxtable. The rest of this chapter is a gathering of random tips, tricks, thoughts and life lessons with very little transitions between the thoughts. (The Dr. is from a TV show – the Cosby Show that ran from 1984 to 1992)

When I watched Dr. Huxtable show Theo how to shave, it hit me that life is full of such rites of passage, and not everyone experiences them in the usual ways. These rituals may seem basic, but they lay the groundwork for independent adulthood. While this book won't give you step-by-step instructions for every task, it emphasizes the importance of these skills. Consider taking classes or finding mentors to master these day-to-day activities.

Moving beyond daily tasks, there are vital lessons not often written down. Skills like critical thinking, empathy, and embracing diversity may sound abstract, but they are our anchors. Don't hesitate to seek guidance on these essential life skills. Our lives are a collection of lessons and memories at every stage. But as we step into adulthood, it becomes clear that some essential teachings weren't handed to us. This guide aims to fill that gap.

Life, Don't talk to me about Life.

In life, challenges are unavoidable, but it's crucial to maintain a balanced perspective and avoid letting setbacks embitter your spirit. This also means extending empathy to those who may have succumbed to bitterness, even if their actions seem harmful. Getting stuck in anger and resentment is a pitiable state, one best avoided. Becoming a paranoid android, always looking at the worst side of life, is also no way to go about living, much less getting ahead. (Yes, there are references to both Douglas Adams's Hitchiker's Guide to the Galaxy and Monty Python's Life of Brian.)

Life is full of choices, big and small. The art of decision-making can sometimes feel daunting, with the pressure to make the perfect choice weighing heavily on our minds. But when you find yourself at a crossroads, instead of overthinking, trust your instincts. Sometimes, to make the right decision, a little creative thinking is in order. Try envisioning the future with each option you're considering. What will life look like in a year, two, or even ten years down the road if you take that path? Envision the Risk versus the Reward. If you can see a positive outcome in your imagination, it's more likely to be the right choice for you. Trust your instincts, and embrace the power of creative visualization when making decisions.

Life is also full of things that are not choices, even if we would prefer otherwise. Privilege is a term that often sparks heated discussions in today's society, and it's essential to understand its implications. Privilege refers to the special rights, advantages, or immunities that are granted or available to specific individuals or groups. In itself, having privilege isn't inherently negative; what matters is our awareness and acknowledgment of it. It becomes problematic when someone is oblivious to their own privilege or, even worse, when they deny having it.

Consider that it's a privilege to be in good health, to have the support of two parents, especially where one provides income, and the other can stay at home to care for the family. It's a privilege to live in certain neighborhoods, attend certain schools, or be a member of socially accepted groups based on characteristics such as race, ethnicity, gender, sexual preference, or sexual identity. This privilege is particularly notable when not belonging to these groups carries disadvantages in various situations, like accessing housing, loans, or social services.

Recognizing your own privileges is a significant step toward fostering empathy and fairness in society. Being sensitive to the advantages you possess can lead to actions that help level the playing field for those who lack the same advantages. I have some privileges by appearing white, some from being tall, male and straight. I have some challenges from being pagan, having long hair and being tall, but a bit chubby. We all have privileges and we all face challenges. Using your privilege, especially those you fought hard to get, to support those less fortunate when possible can contribute to a more equitable and compassionate world. It's important to foster a sense of shared responsibility for the well-being of all members of our diverse and inter-connected society.

Both praise and criticism are facets of human interaction. When you're complimented, embrace it with grace, a simple 'thank you' suffices. On the other hand, criticism, when con-structive, can be a powerful tool for growth. Learn to process feedback objectively without letting it erode your self-worth.

When the moment arises, don't hesitate to request that raise. In professional negotiations, especially concerning salary, you're asserting your self-worth. Equip yourself with thorough re-search and data, but always bear in mind, you're not merely dis-cussing a figure; you're negotiating the worth of your expertise and abilities.

Throughout life's journey, you'll undoubtedly encounter valuable lessons on the art of letting go. This wisdom transcends the mere act of release; it extends to recognizing the precise moments when perseverance is warranted and when it's more prudent to reallocate your energies. In this delicate balance be-tween holding on and letting go, one must navigate the intri-cacies of existence with discernment and grace.

While academic milestones are celebrated, life skills are equally, if not more, critical. Whether it's fixing a leak, man-aging your finances, or even cultivating study habits, these skills empower you to navigate life's unpredictability. Seek classes, mentors or a place you can learn by doing to make sure you have these skills when you need them.

Solitude can be both a sanctuary and a challenge. It offers moments of introspection but can also amplify internal struggles. Mindfulness can be a compass during these moments, guiding you to stay anchored. More on this later.

Respect, Emotions and Understanding

Respecting the autonomy and individuality of others is a fundamental principle of a harmonious society. When someone's actions, beliefs, or practices neither harm nor obstruct you or anyone else, it is unjust to pass judgment or, worse, resort to bullying or ostracism. It's essential to recognize that merely holding the belief that another person's practices could potentially result in spiritual harm doesn't constitute harm inflicted upon you or them. In essence, allow people the space to express their true selves, while you, too, have the freedom to be unapologetically yourself. Embracing diversity is a transformative endeavor, but if you find it challenging, at least practice tolerance, and seek your own path to joy and fulfillment.

Understanding the difference between knowing, understanding, and integrating knowledge is essential for personal growth and empathy. Imagine knowing that exercise is important for your health, a mere acknowledgment of its significance. When you stop exercising and start feeling the physical changes, that's when you understand its importance on a deeper level. However, true integration happens when you incorporate exercise into your daily life, making it a habit.

In life, there are certain experiences, such as living with a disability or an invisible chronic condition, that we can grasp intellectually but never truly comprehend without personally going through them. These situations require us to cultivate empathy and compassionate understanding. Empathy involves a deliberate effort to connect with the emotions, difficulties, and experiences of those who face such challenges, even if we haven't experienced them ourselves. This empathetic approach is fundamental to building a more compassionate and understanding society, one where we wholeheartedly support each other through life's diverse trials.

As we engage with those facing such conditions, it's important to express our willingness to learn and assist. Acknowledging our inability to fully understand their experiences, we can say, "I know you have this particular challenge, but I can't fully comprehend it. Please bear with me as I try to learn how best to help and not hinder you." This simple act of honesty and willingness to support is a step toward creating a more inclusive and compassionate community.

Morality, often intertwined with religious beliefs, sparks debates regarding its connection to faith. Some insist that religious guidelines are a prerequisite for a moral compass, yet the essence of morality transcends religious teachings. At its core, morality entails a fundamental understanding of right and wrong, a concept accessible beyond the confines of religious doctrines. Numerous secular individuals exemplify strong moral values, consistently demonstrating compassion, empathy, and fairness in their actions. It's imperative to acknowledge the multifaceted nature of morality, shaped by personal convictions, societal norms, and individual experiences, and not restricted to the realm of religious faith. Embrace the diversity of beliefs, refrain from judgment, and respect individual choices, whether they involve faith or its absence. Guard against external pressures that seek to compromise your personal religious practices or coerce you into religious observance.

Exercise caution when a preacher advises on voting or a politician guides your prayers; true integrity respects the sacred boundaries between faith and politics.

Sexuality remains a sensitive topic in many cultures. Preconceived notions can lead to misconceptions, biases, and, at times, outright discrimination. Sexuality is an intrinsic part of human nature. It's a spectrum, and individuals may identify anywhere along this continuum. It's crucial to approach the topic with an open mind, free from biases. Understand that each individual's journey and experiences are unique. Accepting and embracing one's sexuality and the sexuality of others without judgment is a step towards a more inclusive and understanding society.

Understanding and regulating our emotions can often be an uphill battle, especially if we haven't had ideal role models. Seeking help or guidance in this realm is not a sign of weakness but a step towards emotional resilience.

That being said, understanding and embracing emotions is a vital aspect of being human. Society often sends overt and subtle messages to ignore, invalidate, bury, and suppress our emotions, but this approach is fundamentally flawed. Emotions, ranging from anger and sadness to joy and excitement, are the core of our human experience. They make us feel alive, infusing depth and color into our thoughts and life experiences. These energetic encounters are not signs of weakness; instead, they are essential components of a healthy and functioning brain.

Emotions are not meant to be stifled; they serve as powerful impulses designed by nature to propel us into action. Fear prompts us to run from danger, anger compels us to fight for survival, and sadness moves us to seek comfort from others. Emotions are, in essence, survival advantages that make our bodies react swiftly to both threats and pleasures. Without excitement, we would lack the motivation to explore new endeavors, and without sexual excitement, the continuation of our species would be in jeopardy.

However, judgment, shame, or abandonment for expressing these core emotions can lead to chronic anxiety or depression. Society's teachings often lead us to suppress emotions, which, in turn, can result in various mental health challenges such as anxiety, depression, PTSD, and personality disorders. These diagnoses are often rooted in the strategies our mind and body employ to cope with overwhelming emotions, especially in cases of abuse or neglect.

Acknowledging and validating our emotions is a crucial step toward better living. By recognizing that fear, sadness, excitement, and joy may be hiding beneath anxiety, we can address the underlying emotions more effectively. For instance, identifying the anger beneath feeling "stepped on" allows us to assert our wants and needs, or, alternatively, to choose not to take further action. Learning to validate our emotions and thoughtfully navigate their expression is an empowering journey that can significantly improve our mental and emotional well-being.

Relationships and Communication

In the realm of relationships, conflicts are inevitable. But it's the manner in which these conflicts are addressed and navigated that truly defines the strength and longevity of a relationship. The frequency of disagreements isn't necessarily a measure of relationship health. Instead, the focus should be on the quality of communication and the strategies employed to resolve differences.

Active listening plays a pivotal role in fostering understanding between partners. It's more than just hearing words; it's about genuinely understanding the emotions and sentiments behind them. When both partners feel heard and validated, it lays the foundation for a constructive conversation and resolution.

Dismissive behaviors, like eye-rolling, sarcasm, or tuning out, can be harmful. They not only hinder effective communication but also undermine trust and intimacy, signaling a lack of respect and widening emotional gaps between partners. Similarly, avoid suppressing your partner's emotions or triggering unnecessary anger—ask first. Questions like "Why did you roll your eyes?" or "What was that reaction about?" show that listening is a two-way street. It is all about two-way, respectful communication.

Many of our relationship behaviors are learned. We unconsciously model our relationships on what we've witnessed in our families, amongst friends, or in media. While some of these modeled behaviors can be positive, others might be unhealthy or dysfunctional.

Recognizing these patterns is the first step. Introspection allows us to understand where our behaviors stem from. But true growth often requires unlearning. It means challenging ingrained beliefs and behaviors and seeking healthier ways of relating and communicating.

Relationships are dynamic, requiring continuous effort and adaptation. While our past provides a blueprint, it's up to us to decide which parts to keep and which to redesign. Embracing positive communication techniques and being open to unlearning can pave the way for deeper connections and fulfilling relationships.

As time marches on, our perception of it evolves. Cherish each fleeting moment, forge memories, and live with purpose. Life isn't a dress rehearsal; it's the main event. If possible, engage with an elder (like me) to discuss the shifts that come with aging. Perspectives alter, reflections on missed youthful opportunities arise, and more. While reminiscing can be comforting, it also offers an opportunity to grasp life's profound lessons at a younger age than it took some of us to truly understand.

Life is an ever-evolving book, and we're both its authors and readers. While this guide provides some hints at the lessons, your experiences will add unique chapters. Embrace the journey, for the voyage of understanding and growth is continuous and boundless.

More on Solitude: The Double-Edged Sword

The stillness of solitude can evoke a myriad of emotions. For some, it's a sought-after sanctuary, a respite from the cacophonies of the bustling world, offering precious moments of reflection and clarity. These quiet intervals can be the birthplace of profound self-awareness, creativity, and rejuvenation. Yet, for others, solitude can also be challenging, almost echoing with its silence, magnifying internal dilemmas, past regrets, or anxious thoughts about the future.

In such moments, when the weight of one's own company becomes overwhelming, the practice of mindfulness can be a beacon. But what exactly is mindfulness?

Mindfulness is the conscious act of focusing one's attention on the present moment, accepting it without judgment. Derived from ancient Buddhist practices, it has been embraced in modern times as a form of meditation, therapy, and everyday practice. Its essence is to engage fully with the present, observing one's feelings, thoughts, and sensations without attempting to change or judge them.

In solitude, mindfulness can be a grounding tool. When internal voices become too clamorous, mindfulness reminds you to anchor yourself in the 'now.' It's like tuning into a radio frequency that plays the rhythmic pulse of your heartbeat, the cadence of your breath, or the subtle sensations of the air against your skin. By turning your attention to these simple present moments, you're often able to quiet the chaos, transforming solitude from a challenge into a comforting embrace.

Moreover, regular mindfulness practices, such as meditation or deep breathing exercises, can equip you with skills to navigate solitude with grace. It's about training the mind to find serenity amidst the stillness and seeing solitude not as isolation but as an opportunity to reconnect with oneself.

While solitude has its dual facets, equipped with mindfulness, one can chart a path through its depths, discovering treasures of insight, self-assurance, and inner peace along the way.

Walk Against Traffic, Not With It

Walking on the road can sometimes be unavoidable, especially in areas where sidewalks or footpaths are absent. It's vital to understand the best practices for your safety in such situations.

One of the most essential rules when walking on the road is to always walk against traffic. This means that you should be facing oncoming cars. Why is this so crucial?

Visibility: When you walk facing oncoming traffic, you can see vehicles approaching you. It allows you to anticipate and react accordingly, whether that means moving further to the side or signaling the driver.

Reaction Time: If a vehicle is coming too close or isn't slowing down, seeing it approach gives you a better chance to react quickly, potentially preventing an accident.

Awareness: Drivers are more likely to see you if you're facing them. When walking with the flow of traffic, vehicles approach from behind, and drivers may not notice a pedestrian until the last second, especially if they're driving at higher speeds or are distracted.

Remember, roads are designed primarily for vehicles, not pedestrians. Cars, trucks, and other vehicles are powerful machines that, even at low speeds, can cause significant harm.

As a pedestrian, you don't have the protection of an exterior frame or safety features like airbags. As candidly put, humans are, in essence, "squishy meat sacks" in comparison to the metal machines that are vehicles.

Walking on roads requires you to be hyper-aware of your surroundings. Here are a few additional tips:

Avoid Distractions: Don't wear headphones or focus too intently on your phone. You need all your senses to navigate the road safely.

Wear Visible Clothing: Especially if walking during dawn, dusk, or nighttime, wearing reflective or brightly colored clothing can make a significant difference in your visibility.

Plan Ahead: If you know you'll be walking on roads frequently, consider mapping out the safest route or investing in safety gear like reflective vests or LED armbands.

Working with Computers

As an IT engineer, I'll naturally be providing some tips and tricks for using your computer. I'm also old, so this isn't about Smartphones or VR stuff. First and foremost, avoid cluttering your PC's desktop with files. This seemingly harmless practice can actually slow down your computer's performance since everything on the desktop loads into your computer's memory. Instead, employ the use of shortcuts to the files you need while keeping the actual files stored in organized folders such as "Documents." This simple tweak can enhance your computer's speed and responsiveness.

Another valuable technique to have in your IT toolkit is the "Undo" command, activated by pressing Ctrl+Z. This keyboard shortcut serves as a digital safety net, allowing you to swiftly correct mistakes while editing documents or performing various tasks. "Undo" can be a lifesaver, preventing potential mishaps and saving you from the frustration of rework.

Moreover, if you find yourself straining to read text in your windows, there's a handy shortcut to adjust the text size. By holding down the Windows key and simultaneously pressing the Plus (+) key, you can easily zoom in on the content, making it more legible. Conversely, pressing the Minus (-) key can quickly reduce the text size. These keyboard shortcuts are not only convenient but also effective in customizing your computing environment to your preference, ultimately enhancing your digital efficiency.

By selectively choosing which applications to run at startup, you can significantly improve your computer's boot time and overall performance. Open your task manager with a simple keyboard shortcut, Ctrl + Shift + Esc. Once in the task manager, navigate to the "startup" tab. Here, you can configure which programs launch automatically when your system boots up. This fine-tuning can help ensure that your system operates more efficiently and allows you to focus on your tasks rather than dealing with unnecessary software running in the background.

The Rules of the Road

Here's another piece of advice, particularly relevant coming from a driver who might occasionally wear the hat of a "grumpy driver." Understanding and adhering to traffic rules is essential for smooth and safe travel. I was, for one of my many jobs, a professional driver - over the road, 48 states and Canada, so perhaps I have seen a bit more of the advantages of the rules of the road than some. On the interstate, you'll notice that the rightmost lane is designed for slower-moving vehicles or those exiting the highway. Each lane to the left of that rightmost lane is meant for passing. If you find yourself not passing other vehicles, it's a good practice to move to the right. If you ever notice that other vehicles are passing you on your right, it's a sign that you might be driving too slowly for your current lane, and it's courteous to shift right.

Let's talk about on-ramps too. On-ramps serve the purpose of allowing vehicles to accelerate to the speed of the interstate traffic. When you're driving in the right lane and see a vehicle merging from an on-ramp, you don't have an obligation to move to the left to "let them in." Those merging onto the interstate should ideally be ready to blend with the traffic flow by the time they reach the main road. Shifting left into faster-moving lanes just to accommodate them can disrupt the flow and is generally discouraged. That being said, if there is no faster moving traffic to your left, go ahead and let them in. Always be aware of all the traffic around you, and act accordingly.

"Letting other people go" may appear to be the polite or friendly thing to do, but few who practice this take the greater number of people they greatly inconvenience into account. Many times this practice serves to only slow down everyone, as you are breaking the normal flow of traffic, breaking the rules of the road, and causing confusion to everyone else. This is not to say you should never be courteous, but exercise caution and prudence when doing so. For example, once I left a gap for someone to get out of a parking lot on my right. They were turning left instead of right - and unfortunately took my gap, getting hit broadside by the car coming in the other lane on my left. The cop said it wasn't my fault and told me to go on my way - but the feeling of responsibility for my "kindness" didn't quickly fade.

In essence, mastering traffic laws and adhering to best practices contributes to the efficiency and safety of our roadways. While it's true that not everyone follows these rules, the more drivers who do, the smoother and more organized our collective driving experience becomes.

The Art of Critical Thinking

Always question any and all information you come across. Challenge it. What's the main idea? How is this idea supported, and what evidence backs it up? Learn the knack of sizing up information sources. Are they reliable? Is there a potential bias? Look into the author's qualifications, the publication source, and possible conflicts of interest. See things from various angles. Delve into opposing viewpoints. What evidence supports each perspective? Dig into the assumptions underlying arguments or statements. Are they valid, and how do they shape the overall argument?

Get familiar with common logical fallacies and sharpen your ability to spot them. Watch out for ad hominem attacks - which are arguments against the character or motivations of a person instead of against their position or argument, hasty generalizations, or appeals to emotion. Hone your skill in assessing evidence quality. Is it reliable, relevant, and enough to support the conclusion? Critical thinking is all about problem-solving.

Break down complex issues into manageable parts. What are the crucial components, and how do they connect?

After encountering information, take some time to reflect. What did you learn, and how has it shaped your perspective? Stay open to changing your viewpoint with new evidence. Nurture a mindset that appreciates intellectual flexibility. Seek out discussions where you can articulate your thoughts and listen to others. This not only refines your ideas but also challenges them.

One last thing I will impart - when you find a problem, a common human response is to combat the symptom they can see, which does little to nothing to alleviate the cause of the problem. This is often done in a destructive manner - fight, punish, outlaw, eradicate, etc the symptom, but it would be better for all, and less costly for the most part, to instead attempt to constructively resolve the cause of the symptom that is seen as a problem.

Critical thinking is a skill that grows with practice and exposure to diverse ideas. Cultivate a mindset of inquiry and skepticism while staying open to new information and perspectives. Just try to make sure that you are at least able to think yourself out of a wet paper bag, so you don't get that unflattering reputation.

And, Finally, Writing and Grammar

Communicating through writing is a distinctive trait of the human species. While various animals leave markings to convey messages, humans have evolved language and writing to effectively share ideas. To achieve this, it is essential to grasp and adhere to the rules of writing in our chosen language. Spelling, grammar, and punctuation play a significant role. While it's possible to convey an idea without perfect writing, clarity enhances communication. The easier it is for your reader to understand, the more likely they are to engage with your words and give them credibility. You may have encountered some challenging words and phrases throughout the book - and this was by intention. It is always good to learn new ways to express your ideas.

Here are some common pitfalls to avoid:

Homophones and Homonyms:
Pay attention to words that sound the same but have different meanings and spellings. For example, "there," "their," and "they're" are often misused. While these words may be interchangeable in speech, in writing, they convey distinct ideas.
Incorrect: "Their going to the park over there."
Correct: "They're going to the park over there."
"Their" is a possessive pronoun, prompting the question "Their WHAT is going to the park?" On the other hand, "they're" is a contraction of "they are."
There are a lot of these in English – Break vs Brake, Right vs Write, Cite vs Site, Allowed vs Aloud. Good written communication requires knowing the differences in their spellings, no matter how alike they sound when speaking. (One site on the resources web page has 300 similar combinations)

Subject-Verb Agreement:

Ensure that your subjects and verbs agree in number. Singular subjects should have singular verbs, and plural subjects should have plural verbs.

Incorrect: "The team are playing well."

Correct: "The team is playing well."

Maintain consistency between subjects and verbs for clear and effective communication.

Apostrophes:

Use apostrophes correctly to indicate possession or contraction. Misplaced apostrophes can change the meaning of a sentence.

Incorrect: "Its a beautiful day."

Correct: "It's a beautiful day."

In the first example, "its" is possessive, implying ownership of the day. The second, with "it's," is a contraction indicating "it is."

Sentence Structure:

Be mindful of sentence structure. Run-on sentences and sentence fragments can confuse your reader.

Incorrect: "She walked to the store she bought groceries."

Correct: "She walked to the store, and she bought groceries."

The first example might cause confusion, prompting the reader to backtrack and decipher the intended meaning: did she buy a store? Where do the groceries come in? The second, with proper punctuation, ensures clarity without extra effort.

Redundancy:

Avoid unnecessary repetition or redundancy in your writing. It can make your message unclear and tiresome to read.

Incorrect: "The reason why he left is because he was unhappy."

Correct: "He left because he was unhappy."

The term "because" signals that a reason is about to be revealed, making "the reason why" redundant.

In online discussions, even amid the heat of an argument, which we all seem to enjoy engaging in, strive to communicate effectively. Clear, well-crafted writing not only conveys your thoughts more persuasively but also earns you credibility and respect in any conversation.

And this wraps up all I can think to convey right at this moment. I greatly appreciate you having read this far. In this life, it is often said that you can be anything you want to be, which, like most things is not as simple as it appears, but as far as it is true, I would encourage you to strive to be happy, be kind, be loving and be loved.

In Peace and Spirit be!

For more resources and links, visit : https://bak9.net/EPR

9

Addendum - Math

Financial math plays a crucial role in making informed decisions about your investments and financial goals. Let's delve into a scenario where a company offers a 4.5% interest rate, but you need to maintain a subscription at \$9.00 per month. The question becomes: How much do you need in that account to cover the subscription fee?

Formula for Simple Interest: $I = P \times r \times t$

Where:

I is the interest earned,

P is the principal amount (initial investment),

r is the annual interest rate (as a decimal),

t is the time the money is invested or borrowed for, in years.

In this case, your monthly subscription fee becomes an annual cost of $9.00×12=$108.00.

Assuming you want the interest earned to cover this cost, rearrange the simple interest formula to find the required principal amount (P):

$$P = \frac{I}{r \times t}$$

Given that the annual interest rate (r) is 4.5%, or 0.045 as a decimal, and assuming you're looking at a one-year period (t=1), you can calculate the necessary principal amount.

$$P = \frac{\$108.00}{0.045 \times 1}$$

$$P = \frac{\$108.00}{0.045}$$

$$P \approx \$2,400.00$$

Therefore, you would need to have approximately $2,400.00 in the account to cover the $9.00 monthly subscription fee based on the given interest rate. And therein lies the trap - you have to keep at least $2,400 in your account, or you are losing money on the deal.

If you want to find out how much interest $1,000 would earn at a 2% interest rate in one year, you can use the simple interest formula:

$I = P \times r \times t$

$I = 1000 \times 0.02 \times 1$

$I = 20$

Therefore, the interest earned on $1,000 at a 2% interest rate over one year would be $20. That is a bit underwhelming, especially when banks are offering .5% interest on accounts - but still, any little bit added is a little bit more than you had last month. Of course, that is simple interest, and these days, interest offered by financial institutions is mostly compounded monthly.

Compound interest is a method of calculating interest on both the principal amount and the accumulated interest from previous periods. In other words, it's interest on interest. The process involves reinvesting the interest earned in each period (compounding), allowing the investment to grow exponentially over time.

The compound interest formula can be expressed as:

$$A = P \times \left(1 + \frac{r}{n}\right)^{nt}$$

Where:

A is the future value of the investment/loan, including interest,

P is the principal amount (initial investment/loan amount),

r is the annual interest rate (as a decimal),

n is the number of times that interest is compounded per unit (t ,

t is the time the money is invested or borrowed for, in years.

Here's a breakdown of the components:

r/n represents the interest rate divided by the number of compounding periods per year.

nt is the total number of compounding periods over the investment's lifespan.

The more frequently interest is compounded, the faster the investment grows. This makes compounding a powerful concept in finance, enabling investors to earn interest not just on their initial investment but also on the interest accumulated over time.

For example, if you have $1,000 invested at an annual interest rate of 5%, compounded quarterly (four times a year) for three years, you'd use the formula to calculate the future value (A) after three years.

$$A = 1000 \times \left(1 + \frac{0.05}{4}\right)^{4\times 3}$$

Now, let's calculate each part step by step:

1. $\frac{r}{n} = \frac{0.05}{4} = 0.0125$
2. $nt = 4 \times 3 = 12$
3. $(1 + 0.0125)^{12} \approx 1.161006$

Now, substitute these back into the main formula:

$$A \approx 1000 \times 1.161006$$

$$A \approx 1161.006$$

So, the future value (A) of the $1,000 investment after three years, compounded quarterly at a 5% annual interest rate, would be approximately $1,161.006.

Understanding the basics of financial math empowers you to make informed decisions about your investments, ensuring that your returns align with your financial goals and obligations.

Some other important formulas:

Loan Repayment:

$$EMI = \frac{P \times r \times (1+r)^n}{(1+r)^n - 1}$$

- Where:
    - *EMI* is the Equated Monthly Installment,
    - *P* is the principal loan amount,
    - *r* is the monthly interest rate (annual rate divided by 12),
    - *n* is the total number of payments (loan term in months).

Future Value of a Series:

$$FV = P \times \left(\frac{(1+r)^{nt} - 1}{r} \right)$$

- Where:
    - *FV* is the future value of a series of cash flows,
    - *P* is the periodic payment,
    - *r* is the interest rate per period,
    - *n* is the number of periods,
    - *t* is the number of time periods.

In financial terms, "a series" refers to a sequence of regular, periodic cash flows. These cash flows can be either inflows (money received) or outflows (money paid) that occur at consistent intervals over time. The intervals could be monthly, quarterly, annually, or any other regular time frame.

The concept of a series is often used in calculations involving annuities or investments where there are consistent cash flows.

This formula calculates the future value of a series of cash flows, considering the compounding effect of interest over time. The series could represent regular contributions to a savings or investment account.

Understanding "a series" is crucial when dealing with financial instruments that involve regular contributions or withdrawals, as it helps in accurately calculating future values, returns, and other financial metrics.

Net Worth: $NetWorth = Assets - Liabilities$ Calculate your assets (what you own) and liabilities (what you owe) to determine your net worth.

Return on Investment (ROI): Calculate the percentage return on an investment.

$$ROI = \left(\frac{Current\ Value - Cost}{Cost} \right) \times 100$$

Budgeting: $Savings = Income - Expenses$ Ensure that your savings (income minus expenses) is positive to maintain financial health.

Understanding and using these formulas can empower individuals to make informed financial decisions.

Useful Terms explained:

Gross Income:

Gross income refers to the total earnings or revenue received by an individual or business before deducting any expenses or taxes. It encompasses all sources of income, including wages, salary, bonuses, interest, dividends, rental income, and any other form of earnings.

Components:

- Wages and Salary: The income earned through employment, including regular pay, overtime, and bonuses.
- Investment Income: Earnings generated from investments, such as interest, dividends, and capital gains.
- Rental Income: Money received from renting out properties or assets.
- Business Income: Profits generated from business operations before deducting business expenses.
- Other Income: Any additional sources of income, like alimony, royalties, or freelance work.

Adjusted Gross Income (AGI):

- Definition: Adjusted Gross Income is an individual's total income from all sources, minus specific deductions such as unreimbursed business expenses, medical expenses, and certain other deductions.
- Importance: AGI is a key figure used to determine taxable income. It reflects a more accurate picture of an individual's financial situation than gross income.

FICO Score:

- Definition: FICO Score is a credit score developed by the Fair Isaac Corporation. It is widely used by lenders to assess an individual's creditworthiness based on their credit history.
- Importance: FICO Scores influence the terms of loans and credit offered to individuals. Higher scores generally result in better loan terms.

Let's contrast Annual Percentage Yield (APY) with the Interest Rate:

- Interest Rate:
  - The interest rate is the percentage of the loan amount or deposit on which interest is calculated. It's the basic rate charged by the lender or offered by the bank for the use of money.
- Annual Percentage Yield (APY):
  - APY, on the other hand, is a more comprehensive measure that includes the effect of compounding on the interest rate. It represents the total interest earned on an investment or deposit over a year, factoring in compounding.

While the interest rate is the base rate at which interest is charged or earned, the APY provides a more accurate reflection of the overall return, considering compounding.

APY is always higher than or equal to the nominal interest rate. The more frequently interest is compounded, the larger the difference between APY and the nominal interest rate.

APY gives a better understanding of the true growth potential of an investment, especially when comparing different financial products.

Example:

- Let's say you have two savings accounts, both offering a 5% nominal interest rate. However, Account A compounds interest quarterly, and Account B compounds interest monthly. Account B would likely have a higher APY because it compounds more frequently.

In summary, while the interest rate is the straightforward percentage applied to the principal amount, the APY accounts for the impact of compounding and provides a more accurate measure of the investment's true annual return.

For more resources and links, visit : https://bak9.net/EPR